CHARLES LETTS · FOUNDED 1796

EARLY LEARNING WITH LETTS
For three- to five-year-olds

Where's Little Brown Bear?

Story by Pie Corbett
Activities by David Bell, Pie Corbett,
Geoff Leyland and Mick Seller

Illustrations by Diann Timms

For Poppy and her little bear

Jenny and Baby were playing indoors.
It was cold outside.

Talk about the different toys shown in the picture.

Name all the red toys.

Look for all the toys with wheels.

Which are the soft toys?

3

Baby wanted to play hide and seek.

What pairs can you see in the picture?

A pair of wellington boots?

A pair of gloves?

Can you sort the shoes into their correct pairs?

How many pairs of shoes are there?

Count how many pairs there are altogether.

Jenny felt sad.

She couldn't find Little Brown Bear.

'Where's Little Brown Bear Mum?'

How does Jenny feel?

Will Baby help look for
Little Brown Bear?

What will Mum do?

Where will they look first?

Have you ever lost a special toy?
How did you feel?

What did you do?

They looked in Jenny's room
– but he was not there.

Look at all the things
in Jenny's room.

How many T-shirts can
you see?
Point to them and count.

How many socks are there
lying on the floor?

Count the soft toys.
How many of them are teddies?

Count out loud together.

What things does Jenny have in her
room that you have in yours?

They looked under the stairs
– but he was not there.

Why don't you play
'Hunt the teddy'?

First, find a favourite
cuddly toy.

Take it in turns to hide the toy.
Give directions to help the
person who is looking.

A long way away from the toy
is 'freezing' – you get warmer
as you get nearer.

You're 'boiling' when the toy
is found.

They looked in the kitchen
– but he was not there.

Jenny and Mum are looking all over the house
to find Little Brown Bear.

Where did they look first?

Where was the second place they looked?

Where was the third place they looked?

This is the fourth place.
Can you guess where they will look next?

As Jenny and Baby look around the house will you
remember where they have looked before?
We don't want them looking in the same place twice.

13

Little Brown Bear was lost.

Can you see Jenny's name?

Can you see any other names?

Can you make your name?

Are there other names you
can make?

What about the names of
people in your family?

What food do you keep in your fridge?
Have a look.

Why do we keep food in a fridge?

Take some little bits of food out of the
fridge (for example, a pat of butter),
cover them up and put them in
a warm room.
Leave them for a few hours. Then look at
them. What has happened?

WATCH OUT You should always
wash your hands before you touch food.

Baby looked in the fridge
– but no luck.

Jenny looked in the cat's basket
– but no luck.

Who is looking in the basket?

Who is looking behind the basket?

Do you think that Little Brown Bear is behind the basket?

What can you see on top of the table?

What is under the table?

Where else in the kitchen could Jenny and Baby look?

Mum looked in the shed
– but no luck.

What can you see in the shed?

Can you see the spade, the rake, the
lawn mower,
the watering can, the hose, the flower
pots?

Can you see Little Brown Bear?

WATCH OUT Don't go into a
shed on your own.
There are things that can hurt
you there.

Jenny looked in the garden
– but no luck.

What has Baby found?

When you next go outside
see how many different creatures
you can find. Look under stones, pieces
of wood, leaves. Do it carefully.

If you find some creatures, look at
them closely.

Are they all the same size?

What colour are they?

Do they have legs or wings?

How do they move – do they crawl,
run, jump or squirm?

Put the stone, piece of wood or leaf
back carefully. Remember it's their
home.

They looked in the bathroom
– but no luck.

What is Baby smiling at?

He can see his reflection.

You can see your reflection in a mirror.
Where else can you see your reflection?

Look at a shiny floor, at a spoon,
at a saucepan, at tiles – where else?

Use a hand mirror to spy on someone
around a corner.

You could play 'The Mirror Game'.
Sit facing each other. One of you must
pretend to be a mirror, so you must do
what the other person does.

They looked in Mum and Dad's room
– but no luck.
Little Brown Bear was lost.

What is Jenny doing?

Draw a picture of
Little Brown Bear.

Write a message on it to tell
people he is lost.

Stick your poster up where it
can easily be seen.

27

It was time to go to the shops.
It was raining.

Mum gave Jenny a cuddle
and put on her coat.

Can you help write
the shopping list when you
next go shopping?

Try to think of things
you need.

You could draw or write the
things on the list.

29

'Come on Jenny –
put on your boots.'

What did Jenny feel inside the boot?
Can you tell what something is by just feeling it?

Find ten interesting things and put them into a bag
made from material or a pillow case. Take turns
to put both your hands inside the bag. Try to guess
what each object is. Take it out of the bag to check
your guess. Try doing it again but only put one
hand in.

Which was the most difficult thing to guess?
Have a good look at it. What's it like?
Is it smooth, rough, round, hard, soft . . .
What other words could you use?

Activity notes

Pages 2–3   Children need to be able to distinguish one item from another before they can count them. Sorting activities give them practice in doing this and there are lots of opportunities around the home for sorting household objects, eg cutlery, clothing, toys.

Pages 4–5   Being able to match objects and words is important when children begin to count. Pairing activities help them to understand that one object goes with another. There are lots of things around the home that can be sorted into pairs, such as socks, shoes, matching tops and trousers.
The card game Pairs is another enjoyable way to practise this skill.

Pages 6–7   This activity encourages children to talk about feelings and about what might happen next in the story. This helps to develop an understanding of how stories are structured and the likely sequence of events.
Try asking questions like these with other stories you read together.

Page 8–9   Counting is best done when children are able to point and count out loud. It is even better if they are able to count real things at home, so that they can then move each item away from the rest when it has been counted. It is also helpful if children begin by counting the same kind of objects, for example, counting a number of apples or the family's gloves.

Pages 10–11   Hiding games, which all children enjoy, can help them learn to follow and to give clear instructions. Ask your child to teach you the rules or instructions of a game that they play with their friends.

Pages 12–13   This activity helps to develop the idea of sequence. There are other things you can do at home which involve a number of simple steps over a short period of time, such as preparing food or planting seeds. Talk about the different steps with your child and encourage the use of words like 'firstly', 'secondly'.

Pages 14–15   This activity helps children to pick out letters that matter. Most children learn to recognise their own names fairly easily. Write your child's name as a label – also on letters, cards, on their pictures, etc.
Magnetic letters are a good idea – but try to find lower case ones (not capital letters), as most writing is done with them.

Pages 16–17   Understanding how natural things change is an important part of science. Change takes place at different rates and may not be immediately obvious. You'll need to look closely for changes in colour, shape and texture. Look together at the way ice changes. Put ice cubes on saucers in different places around the home. Which melts the most quickly?

Pages 18–19   Using positional words such as 'inside', 'outside', 'under' and 'over' helps to develop an early understanding of physical space. Encourage your child to use similar words when playing hiding games or looking for something.

Pages 20–21   Children like playing this sort of naming game with a book. At a very young age they enjoy looking at pictures and pointing to familiar objects. This helps to focus their attention on looking for clues and details. You can do this with most picture books.

Pages 22–23   This activity encourages careful observation and helps to develop children's understanding of living things: how they differ, where they live and the importance of treating them with care.
You could continue to observe the creatures in one particular spot near to home. What changes does your child notice? Try other places, such as parks or woods, for different kinds of creatures.

Pages 24–25   Encourage your child to talk about how their reflection changes when they look at different surfaces. What looks most like them? What gives a distorted image?
Look for other reflective surfaces when you are out with your child.

Pages 26–27   Children love to draw their own posters. Ask your child to write down the words. This may come out as a scribble – just write your own version next to theirs. If you do this often you'll notice that the scribble begins to look more and more like letters. Pin the posters up when they are finished.

Pages 28–29   Look for opportunities to share real writing tasks with your child – lists, cards, notices, labels, calendar entries, etc. At first small children will just copy you and scribble. Soon their shapes will look more like letters. When your child has good control over a pencil, show them how to write their own name.

Pages 30–31   This helps children to develop their sense of touch and to think carefully about everyday objects, their shape, texture, etc. It also helps to extend vocabulary, as your child will need to choose the most accurate words to describe what they feel.
You could play this game again, but this time why not make all the objects the same shape or texture?